WHERE AM I?

RIDDLES FOR KIDS

GAIL BOWLING

To order additional copies of this book, contact:
Xlibris
844-714-8691
www.Xlibris.com
Orders@Xlibris.com

Library of Congress Control Number: 2022910910
ISBN: Softcover   978-1-6698-2911-9
         Hardcover   978-1-6698-2912-6
         EBook   978-1-6698-2910-2

Print information available on the last page

Rev. date: 07/19/2022

YOU RIDE IN ME TO SCHOOL MOST DAYS CHATTING WITH YOUR FRIENDS
I'M A BIG, YELLOW KID-MOBILE WHERE THE NOISE NEVER ENDS

I HAVE CANNED AND BOXED FOOD ITEMS STOCKED ON MY SHELVES
YOU CAN EVEN BUY COOKIES SOME SAY MADE BY ELVES

WHEN YOU ARRIVE HERE BRING A NAMED LUGGAGE TAG
BECAUSE WHEN YOU FLY OUT YOU MUST STORE YOUR BAG

THIS HOUSE IS IN BRANCHES SO BRING A STRONG LADDER
IF YOU WANT TO PLAY BRING TREATS AND SOME WATER

WHETHER CAFÉ OR DINER YOU COME HERE TO EAT
SOMETHING THAT'S YUMMY WHETHER SALTY OR SWEET

WHEN YOU COME TO MY WATERS TO SWIM, FISH OR BOAT
BRING A FLOATY DEVICE OR YOU'LL SINK AND NOT FLOAT

WHEN YOU COME TO THIS SHOP IT'S ALL ABOUT HAIR
YOU'LL BE CUT, CURLED, AND FLUFFED BY SOMEONE WITH FLAIR

I HAVE MANY FINE STORES IN A GIGANTIC SPACE
YOU CAN SHOP, EAT OR WALK, BUT SLOWLY, DON'T RACE

WITHIN MY GATES YOU CAN VISIT CREATURES GREAT AND SMALL
ELEPHANTS, MONKEYS, LIONS AND MORE, EVEN GIRAFFE'S SO VERY TALL

YOU CAN RIDE IN MY SWINGS OR THE MERRY-GO-ROUND
BUT GO SLOW ON THE SLIDE OR YOU'LL HIT THE GROUND

YOU PURCHASE YOUR TICKETS AND A SAVORY TREAT
AND WATCH MY BIG SCREEN FROM A COMFORTABLE SEAT

ON THIS FIELD IF YOU HEAR IT'S ONE, TWO, THREE STRIKES YOU'RE OUT
YOU KNOW A PESKY UMPIRE IS LURKING THERE ABOUT

I CARRY SURFERS AND BOATS AND SHIPS TOO
SOME WORK AND SOME PLAY ON MY DEEP WAVY BLUE

YOU COME TO THIS OFFICE WHEN YOU'RE HURT OR ILL
YOU MAY GET A SHOT, BUT, MORE OFTEN A PILL

HERE YOU ZOOM ON STEEL BLADES AROUND AN OPEN SPACE
LIVELY MUSIC BLASTED LOUD MAKES YOU WANT TO RACE

YOU COME HERE FOR CHILLS AND THRILLS OFTEN AT A FAIR
WHETHER ROLLER COASTER OR FERRIS WHEEL IT'S EXCITING THERE

WE SELL ADORNMENTS IF YOU WANT A RING
BUT A COLORFUL NECKLACE MAY BE YOUR THING

ON MOTHERS DAY YOU COME TO ME TO GET A FRAGRANT GIFT
THE PRETTY COLORS AND NICE SMELLS WILL GIVE YOUR MOM A LIFT

I HAVE BENCHES FOR SITTING AND SOFT GRASS FOR PLAY
WHERE YOU CAN TOSS FRISBEES ON A CLEAR, WINDLESS DAY

MY STEEPLE IS HIGH AND MY WINDOWS ARE STAINED
LESSONS INSIDE COME FROM SOMEONE ORDAINED

Printed in the United States
by Baker & Taylor Publisher Services